HOW TO GET THROUGH GRIEF AND GAIN HAPPINESS

Change Your Moment Change Your Life

SHELBY DONER

Dedication

Dedicated to helping all those dealing with loss and grief.
May your life be filled with healing, peace, joy, abundance,
love, prosperity, good health, spirituality, and passion.

Contents

Good Grief, Bad Grief...
What Is Grief?

First off, let us lay out a simple definition of grief since it can be a little tricky. Grief is a unique and normal response to loss of any kind. Grieving is learning how to live with what you lost. A person may experience grief for years and multiple times in their life. Many people are fooled to believe that a person only experiences grief after another beloved person dies. This is so not true. Someone doesn't have to only die for you to undergo grief! And guess what, even animals grieve, believe it or not! There are more times in a person's life than you think where they are unconsciously experiencing grief. However, many call it something else or don't quite know how to deal with it properly.

Grief may be experienced before, during and after an event of loss. And please remember, it is all completely normal. When I say normal, I am talking about you. What you feel, what you think and what you do are all normal reactions for you. Don't be ashamed or think you are weird. You are just being you, so be you in the process. Also, please, don't compare your reactions and losses to other people's or try to copy exactly what they did to heal. One must learn to get to know themselves and find ways to heal that best meet their personal needs. Grief is just as much of a process as healing and recovery is. A person's mindset, personality and living situation are key determinants to their responses to life's events. Below are some life events and conditions where grief may be experienced;

- Accidently causing harm to someone else
- Aging
- Becoming pregnant
- Before and after a surgical procedure
- Being betrayed or lied to
- Being offended by a spouse, friend or other human
- Believing you lost
- Believing you have less
- Believing you will never get what you want
- Breakups
- Cancer diagnosis
- Change in health condition
- Change of another's health condition
- Child moves away
- Child, spouse or other family member sickness
- Chronic illness

- Coming home from college for the summer

- Coming home from a vacation

- Committing a felony or wrong doing

- Comparing self to others

- Crime

- Death of a loved one or animal

- Divorce

- Feeling not good enough

- Feeling unloved

- Feeling unworthy

- Feelings of emptiness or no purpose

- Failing to meet academic, society, personal or job expectations

- Friend, spouse or family conflicts

- Gaining weight

- Getting an abortion

- Going through detoxification

- Hating one's self or life

- Have a baby

- Home environment

- Job environment

- Job loss

- Life transitioning

- Losing a game

- Losing fame

- Losing fortune

- Losing weight

- Making a mistake

- Moving away

- Not getting what you want

- Preoccupation of a particular thought or belief

- Regret

- Retirement

- Self-esteem and personal opinion about one's own identity

- Selling a house, car or other personal item

- Traumatic event

- World terrorist attack

- While being in a depressive state

- While transitioning from single to married

It is very important to understand that there is no such thing as "a correct way to grieve" nor a correct way of "when" to grieve. People grieve in many different ways and most are acceptable. When ideas of suicide, self or others harm are in mind, help should be sought immediately. Those are not acceptable. We are in this world together and have to keep in mind no matter how disconnected we may feel, we are not alone. Grieving can be a whirlwind of emotional, physical, mental, spiritual, behavioral, social and cultural responses and feelings. Listed below are some emotions, symptoms and responses a person may experience while facing grief;

- Abusive behaviors

- Acceptance

- Anger

- Annoyance

- Anxiety

- Avoidance

- Body aches

- Bowel dysfunction

- Cessation of normal hobbies and daily activities

- Change in personality

- Crying

- Decreased self-esteem

- Denial

- Depression

- Detattachment

- Discouragement

- Disordered eating

- Disordered emotions

- Disordered moods

- Disordered sleep

- Disordered thinking

- Extreme fear

- Fatigue

- Frustration

- Greed

- Guilt

- Hair loss

- Hallucinations

- Hatefulness

- Heart palpitations

- Heartache

- Homicide

- Hopelessness

- Hyperventilation

- Increase in irritable moods

- Isolation

- Jealousy

- Lack of desire

- Lack of energy

- Lack of passion

- Lack of positive emotions

- Lack of purpose

- Lack of social interaction

- Laughing

- Loneliness

- Loss of ability to feel emotions

- Loss of connection to life

- Loss of libido

- Midlife crisis decision making

- Muscle pain

- Negative thoughts

- Night sweats

- Numbness

- Odd dreams

- Onset of chronic illness

- Other's neglect

- Panic attacks

- Paranoia

- PTSD

- Rage

- Sadness

- Self-harm

- Self-neglect

- Shaking

- Shame

- Skin rashes

- Stomach pain

- Stress

- Suicide

- Unusual urges and desires

- Weakened immune system

- Weight gain or loss

And who said grief was only five stages long? Please, do not put yourself in a box or try to generalize your grief experience. Be cautious to let a theory on grief or another person determine what "stage" you are in or how you should be feeling. What if I told you there was no such thing as "stages" in grief? The severity, duration and frequency of grief depends on the individual. Every individual and every experience is unique. The only person who truly knows how you feel is you. It is important even when we are not at our best, to keep in mind everything out there is just tools for us to use on our journey to healing. We have the choice to take it or leave it. Use what works best for you and listen to those whom you trust and have faith in. Also, I bet they didn't tell you, you'd experience some positive emotions too along the way. During the grieving period, it is normal to experience unexpected and expected emotions like peace, joy, love, inspiration, gratefulness, respect and honor. Grief can be a constant up and down hill battle of positive and negative emotions colliding and competing for the top. The question is, who are you going to let win?

Together, we must change the stigma of a grieving person. Instead of holding it all together and being alone like society tells you to do, we need to let it all out! Society trains us to only display the good emotions and keep the negative ones to ourselves. In times of grief, I am not sure who is more uncomfortable, the grieving person or society. As a whole, we don't handle loss well. We don't handle our negative emotions well. We freeze, become avoidant, silent or like to change the subject. I have a question for you however, what is wrong with having negative emotions? If you look at the bigger picture, I believe they are no different than positive emotions. They come from the same place and we use the same heart to feel them. The only difference between all emotions is their frequency and tune. They are natural emotions we all experience as human beings. We are more alike than we are different. Don't be afraid to express them when the time comes. It is just you being human and I promise, by doing so, you will be one step closer to seeing the light again. Sometimes we have to dance with what makes us and others uncomfortable. Sometimes we have to just jump into the unknown. I am sure you have heard, "What doesn't kill you makes you stronger." Have faith my friend, you can survive this. It may feel like no one has ever been in your situation or you are not going to overcome this, but this is a false belief. We must find understanding that so many others have been in similar situations as us and have survived. The road that got us to our grief may be different, but the feelings and the thoughts we experience are shared. We are not alone.

What really matters and makes the difference, however, is what you do with the emotions and thoughts as they arise. How you respond and use positive and negative emotions ultimately determines the quality of your life. We must learn to stop running from our emotions and thoughts. In times of loss, questions like these should be considered; Does expressing the emotion harm or serve me? What about life, does it hurt it or make it thrive?

Society is just not used to people displaying negative and suffering emotions. We lock up, push them away, distract ourselves and try to do everything to avoid feeling them. I am here to tell you feeling positive and negative emotions are both very healthy. However, it is important to understand emotions and thoughts are not the same thing and most importantly, you are not your emotions nor your thoughts! Emotions are not intellectual. They come from the heart. They are what animate and give livelihood to our lives. Emotions are the fuel that give vitality and passion to our dreams, hopes, ambitions and beliefs. Without them, every experience in life would be the same, empty and without feeling. Our emotions can be compared to an orchestra. They give melody, beauty, detail and meaning to every event in our lives.

Emotions may be uncomfortable at first, but that is just like learning anything for the first time. Once you've done it and experienced it, it gets a little easier to handle. You just have to take a step back for a moment and realize it. Thoughts and what you think, come from the mind. They are what express and describe the emotions coming up as we analyze what's happening in front of us. With all that being said, grief is truly a holistic experience. Emotions are actually the foundational surface for life itself. They are what make life so beautiful.

It is extremely important in life to master the skill of looking within. We must all learn how to appropriately observe our emotions and thoughts as they come up and identify as to why they are coming up. Then secondly, learn how to control them and how we respond and act to them. Learning how to face how we feel and then how to express it to others and life outside of us is something we all need to work on. We must know where we are coming from. For example, many of us are guilty of acting out of a state of anger. Maybe we said something we didn't mean or did something we regret the second we did it. My question for you is, did anger cause us to do that or did some other emotion cause this? For many of us, anger is never really the true source of this event. Emotions such as fear, hurt and stress tend to be the root cause of it all. For many, anger is just the outward expression of the hidden emotion fueling it all. Once we realize this and understand this trait about ourselves, we are one step closer to getting out of the darkness.

Holding everything in only makes us suffer more. As a society, we must stop making it such an intellectual journey. Full acceptance, instead of trying to change the emotion, is needed. Just 'thinking' our way through our grief is not enough for us if we want to recover fully. The heart knows what it wants and exposes to us how it feels. We must learn to listen to it and accept what it is expressing. Then experience what it is expressing and carefully use the mind to choose the next best step. When I say step, I mean action that will serve you and the greater good.

Grief is not immediately learning how to fix yourself and life, but more so about learning how to accept what has taken place outside of you and what you are feeling because of it. Grief is not meant to be pain free. There will be pain and suffering. Where there is love, there too, will be grief. Loss can affect us in so many different ways. It affects us physically, mentally, emotionally, financially, relationally, spiritually and even alters our present and future. For example, when someone dies, we lose the physical connection we once had. We are no longer able to hug them or hear their voice. On the emotional level when they die, we are left with only memories to stimulate certain feelings within us. As a society, we must learn to be honest and accept loss for what it is. We must learn how to cope with it as it arises in our lives and how to nurture ourselves effectively so that we may thrive once again after it has occurred. Everyone here on earth has or will experience loss at some point in their life. It is inevitable. Grief recovery if you want to call it that, requires testing our belief systems. How we believe we should feel during or after a time of loss, ultimately determines our reality and recovery speed. I am here to tell you, don't be afraid to explore. Sometimes our ideas and beliefs about loss and grief can be a little misleading. Don't be afraid to bring them to the surface because false ideas can lead to false feelings and ultimately, failure to thrive. Be brave and seek the truth to the naturalness and realness of what you are feeling. Challenge them and I promise, you will find understanding.

People don't realize how much the quality of a person's life is impacted when loss occurs. They normally are neither mentally or physically prepared for it when it hits. How we feel, what we think and what we do, determine how we respond to life when it unfolds in front of us. Who we are and what we believe, determine the meaning we give to life. The fulfillment, love, joy, passion and happiness we all long for in life is found from within. Grief is not a disease nor is it a psychotic disorder. It is just a part of life. Everything in life has a cause and an effect. There are forces of good and evil. No matter what happens in our lives, the universe continues to have a plan of its own. Life keeps going even if it feels like ours has stopped. God gave us emotions so we could feel, thoughts so we could think and free will so we could act. The ultimate experience of our life is in our own hands. The outside world and everything happening outside of us may be out of our control, but the inside world, it is in our full control. We get to choose how the outside world affects us and how we will respond to it. Many people today suffer from their grief and do not take the necessary actions to get the help they need to improve their life. For many, they are trying to control something they never truly had control of in the first place. We all come from a place of innocence and have to remember we are in this together. On the other side during loss and really life in general, people innocently get stuck believing their life is less. People unconsciously and consciously choose to accept their life for what it is. They choose to live a life of suffering. After an abnormal or negative event, many begin to believe they will never get what they want. Their mind convinces them they lost everything and will never get it back.

We must learn how to change these words, "loss, less and never," that fill so many people's minds. Instead in their place, we need to focus on using the words "gain, more, and always." We may not be able to control life, but the one thing we can control is how we respond to it. No one wants to suffer their entire lives and I believe we all truly come from a place of good. We have the power to turn our attention to the belief that our life is more and we have so much more to gain. We each were put here on earth for a reason. Our life was a gift given to us. As long as we are still alive, there is always time to make it better and end our suffering. There is always time to be happy. We are solely responsible for how we feel and what we do in the end. Instead of blaming, when loss happens and grief begins, we must look at our reactions. There is a purpose for everything, especially for you.

You may not be able to control the rain when it rains, but you can control how you respond to it. It is possible to become unshakable in the rain and more importantly, a hero instead of a victim in your circumstances. Everyone has the opportunity to write and change their life story.

Being impacted by grief, it is my duty to help end suffering from grief for humanity. I want to stop loss from ruining people's precious lives. I am here to serve others and help people learn how to improve their quality of life. I truly believe obtaining bliss, freedom, and love for one's life is possible for anyone. The remainder of this short book is how I transformed my moment and my life. I may push you at times and make you feel somewhat uncomfortable, but it is all for the greater good. This book contains quick and easy steps anyone can incorporate into their daily life. I got through grief and gained tremendous happiness using these simple tasks. Today, I can say undoubtedly, I love my life. I promise you, if you implement these you can change your life too!

Dare to Become Aware

One Step At A Time

The first step in conquering grief is becoming aware of the unaware. In order to do that, you must begin to ask yourself questions and look within. You must become the questioner and the answerer. Instead of being stuck in our negative and debilitating state, we must begin to ask why, what, where and how. It is important to become aware of the thoughts that fill our minds, the emotions we feel inside and the actions we do on a daily basis. Acknowledging these require genuine self honesty, courage and strength. If we lived in a completely unconscious state, how do you think life would be? Do you think we would be able to change, advance or grow as human beings? When we consciously ask questions, that is where the healing and beauty begins. The unconscious must be brought into the conscious mind. Once it is brought into our awareness, we can then take the steps to change our lives. We have to ask ourselves why we do, why we feel and why we think what we do. It all has to come from some source. Our job is to find it! Insight and understanding to our problems, suffering and pain can all be found. And once we find it, we will know what step to or not to take. More importantly, by becoming more aware, it can give us hope and a new sense of direction for our lives. The power to heal ourselves and obtain a better life is found from within. Recognizing that you are grieving is the key to the path of happiness. Below are life transforming questions to consider asking yourself;

- What do I spend most of my time focusing on?

- Who am I? What do I think of myself as a person?

- What does life mean to me?

- What am I doing with my life?

- Do I love my life?

- Do I want to live like this forever?

- What do I want out of life?

- Where do I want to be in 1 year, 5 years, 10 years?

- How am I going to get out of life what I want?

- How can I add more value to my life?

- How can I become a better human being?

- How do I treat other people?

- Do I want to be happy?

- Am I suffering? If so, do I want to stop suffering?

- What emotions am I feeling on a consistent basis? Why am I feeling them?

- What thoughts consume my thinking? Are they positive, negative or neutral?

- How does my body feel right now?

- What needs to be changed in order for me to be happy? What do I have to do? What has to happen?

- Do I need help?

- What can I do to change the way I feel?

- How can I begin to think more positively?

- What do I need to work on? What could I do better or improve on?

- Is there anything holding me back?

Become A Better Caretaker

Your Life Matters

In times like these, it is important to take care of yourself even if you don't want to. It seems contradictory, but when we are at our weakest, we must be our strongest. You must force yourself to make the health of your mind, body and soul a priority. It is in the nurturing that our broken hearts begin to heal. Grieving can place large amounts of stress on the body and mind. It is a very physical, mental and emotional experience. If one is not properly equipped to handle such an intensity, future health is put at risk. Problems can arise for you if sufficient attention is not given.

For example, the death of my father was unexpected. It was traumatic, heartbreaking and hit me like a sledgehammer. It threw me into a dark place where I put my health in jeopardy. I developed an eating disorder, went into depression, developed an odd skin disorder, had fertility issues, hair loss, and even suicidal thoughts. Instead of seeking help, I put a lot of unnecessary stress and harm in my body and today, I am paying for it. The last thing I want is for a situation of loss to do that to you. Health must not be ignored or taken for granted.

Have you ever heard the old saying, "time heals everything" or been told, "It will be okay, just give it time"? What if I told you we had it all wrong? The amount of time that passes is not the secret ingredient to recovering from grief. What we do with the time is actually the secret ingredient to healing. Time must take on a whole new view. If you think about, what good does it do for us to just sit around and "wait to get better"? Many people live with broken hearts expecting that eventually over time they will heal. How does one get better during that process if nothing is done?

Unfortunately, grief is not like a wound that can normally heal itself on its own. Grief and loss are more like breaking a leg. When you break a leg you don't just wait around and expect it to miraculously get better do you, you go to the doctor for help! Working as a nurse, I have had the privilege to assist a very kind doctor set many broken leg bones. Healing after breaking a bone is a process just like grief. If we want to heal and walk again, we must take the right steps to help make that happen. For example, you get an x-ray to see the type and severity of the break. Without it, no doctor will know what he or she is working with or the condition of the patient. That is why this is one of the very first steps taken. As you can see, this is a very similar step to becoming fully aware of what you are thinking, feeling and doing. Then the doctor has to take specific interventions to properly set the bone back into place. These steps are unique to the type of break and person. Sometimes this may require surgery, a lot of ice, ACE wraps, pain control, sedation, medications, rest, physical manipulation or even emotional support. Just like that, dealing with loss can require many interventions. And when I say many interventions, I mean steps that will help you the best.

We are very unique when it comes to our healing processes. Just like the bone, we may all be desiring the same thing, but the road to healing for our specific break, may be different. It is important that we discover what works and doesn't work best for us. We must begin to really get to know ourselves.

Next, after taking the effective interventions, another x-ray is ordered to see if the bone is in proper ailment. They are looking to see if the bone is set properly so it can heal. Reassessment and self-awareness is just as crucial during grief. Broken hearts and people affected by loss must make a conscious effort to reassess during this time in their life. We have to make sure we are on the right road to recover and are "setting" the correct path in order to heal.

If we notice we are a little off, then we will know we need to adjust. Once the bone is properly set, a cast is then carefully placed. A cast is like a set path for healing, when someone finds it, hope for a full recovery is made known.

Along the way, you may require multiple x-rays to see if you are making progress and possibly several recasts to form the new you. However, two things remain true. As you heal from brokenness, time is not in charge of you nor are you fully relying on it. During loss and breaking a leg, what we do within the timeframe from when it happens to now, ultimately determines the amount of healing. Time just becomes a known factor on the road to recovery. I call it patience and before you know it, you won't be running anymore with broken legs. You'll be pain free and your heart will be radiating gold from the inside out. You will be healed, soaring high as you continue to live your life.

Life doesn't wait on time and nor should you! Finding and setting the path is the secret ingredient to your recovery! Below are key recommendations I used to heal and to gain happiness after the loss of my father. Consider incorporating some, if not all of the following into your life today and everyday;

Body

- Make sure to eat a well-balanced diet and to get proper nutrition (Hire a nutritionist if necessary)
- Do not starve yourself or attempt to comfort yourself by overeating

- Make sure to stay hydrated, drink plenty of water (Half your body weight in ounces per day)
- Do not over consume caffeine, sugary, or alcoholic beverages
- Perform deep breathing techniques (Do the 5 by 5 method 1 to 3 times a day-Inhale for 5 seconds, hold for 5 seconds, exhale for 5 seconds, repeat)
- Continue to keep up with your personal hygiene (Showering, brushing your teeth, etc.)
- Make sure to get at least 6-8 hours of sleep (If you struggle with sleeping that long at night, attempt to take at least a 30 minute nap during the day)
- Do not make a habit of sleeping 10 or more hours per night
- Learn how to meditate
- Begin weight training and aerobic exercise (Hire a personal trainer if necessary)
- Continue to be active and social
- Attempt to get at least 20 minutes of sunlight each day
- Continue to do the hobbies you love
- Join a volunteer group
- Get massages (optional)

Mind

- Ask for support or help if you feel you are not okay (A friend, family member, therapist, pastor, etc.)
- Become aware of your thoughts and emotions (Raise your consciousness)
- Become aware if you are fully present in the moment or are thinking about the future or past, observe where your thoughts are
- When grieving-like emotions and thoughts come to the surface and begin to cause physical effects or urges, (Ex. panic attacks, crying, rage, extreme fatigue, not wanting to do anything, etc.) attempt to stay in control and don't be afraid. Let yourself experience them in a controlled and safe manner. Avoid holding back and holding them in
- Meditate
- Pray
- Serve others (Do random acts of kindness, join a nonprofit, help out at a church, school etc.)
- Forgive anyone who has hurt you or done wrong to you
- Observe if you are having any feelings of guilt, blame, or anger. Identify where they are coming from and why. Then what you should do
- Forgive yourself

- Let go of what needs to be let go
- Stop letting the past define you
- Learn to love yourself
- Give yourself permission to move on
- Join a support group online or local community group
- Take steps to live in a beautiful state rather a suffering state
- Believe in yourself
- Smile and laugh every day
- Get a pet
- Spend 10 minutes of your day completely relaxed, be still, be silent
- Immerse yourself in nature
- Spend time with little children
- Surround yourself with people who love you and care about you
- Listen to motivational and peaceful music
- Listen to self-help and motivation podcasts
- Learn something new
- Attempt to live in the present moment
- Thank God everyday for your life
- Give yourself some grace
- Look into the mirror at yourself with love and happiness
- Think about and write down what you are grateful for

- Hang out with people you love
- Read self-help books or books similar to your life situation
- Visualize your goals happening, living the life you desire, and you feeling utter joy and fulfillment (The brain can't tell what is real or imaginative)
- Taking action to think positive, stop doing the things that are holding you back and do what you need to do to get the life you desire
- Look at the loss, face it, relive it and find its truth
- Observe the meaning you are giving the loss and see if it is really true, empowering or disempowering you

Soul

- Realize you are not your thoughts, your emotions, your body or the events happening in your life (You are the soul that uses the thoughts, emotions and body to experience the events in your life. The body and mind do not control you, you control them! You tell the body when to go and what you do. Don't let it or the mind control you.)
- Stop taking life for granted, remember you only live once
- Stop being selfish

- Reflect life is a gift, it was given to you, you did not do anything to earn it nor can we keep anything here forever. With this said, we should look at everything in our lives with a grateful state rather a "I deserve this.." state
- Stop making your life about you and start making it about others
- Do things that awaken your soul
- Remember you are blessed
- Give and contribute to others (The secret to living is giving!)
- Help others in need
- Be there for those who are hurting and in pain
- Pray for others
- Give praise and thanks to our Creator
- Attempt to reach a higher consciousness level
- Challenge yourself and your mindset
- Strive to act with love and kindness
- Be who you are
- Attempt to be the best you can be
- Be greater than your past, trials and tribulations
- Attempt to use every moment for good
- Be present, be one with all

Hello, How Are You?

The Power Of Connection

The power of, "Hello, how are you?" has been forgotten in today's society. As social media has taken over our world, very few are comfortable greeting another human being in person. In person conversations scare the bejeebers out of some people now a days and some can barely make eye contact with others. Genuine connection with others has severely declined over the years and communication has become a struggle. Don't get me wrong, some advancements have been extremely beneficial. How lucky are we that we can contact someone who lives entirely across the word in a second? No waiting for a letter to cross the seas, but I want to ask you, are these connections truly felt and real? Is there love, is there a true connection?

We have developed a pattern of being more comfortable with a cellphone's screen rather than a helping hand, a kind stranger's smile or a loved one's hug. In times of sadness or during any other negative feeling, one of the first things we do as a society is pull out our phones. With a touch of a finger, we are drawn away and distracted from our personal problems. We become lost in other people's online reality hoping it will make us feel better, but in all reality, it just causes us deeper damage inside. If healing is to take place in times of loss, proper human to human communication is absolutely required. We must be the same person we are offline that we are online with ourselves and with others.

It is essential to become comfortable in the uncomfortable. I challenge you to take the next opportunity to authentically greet a loved one or a complete stranger. Put your best interest in fully engaging and listening to what they have to say. Not only does this help you, but you never know who you may be helping heal. Everyone is fighting their own battle we know nothing about. We shouldn't expect them to know how we feel or know what we think every moment. We must learn to fully express ourselves and tell them.

If you desire to heal, real connection and love with another is a must. For example, by simply doing an act of kindness, it allows you to stop focusing on yourself momentarily. Our survival depends on connection with others. In order to thrive, we must give and receive love. We needed it to survive as newborns and toddlers and will continue to need it as older adults. Conversations with others can give you new insight to your situation and lead you to a whole different meaning for your life. Speaking from experience, you might even realize your life hasn't been as bad as you thought it has been. By hearing someone else's story, it can give you the hope and strength you need to conquer whatever you may be facing. And lastly, you might just meet a new lifelong friend, a friend who helped you through your worst time and stuck by your side through it all. Be the hello to a stranger and please consider limiting your screen time.

Please Don't Take Your Life For Granted

The Time Is Now

Sometimes life is extremely hard. It can cause tremendous heartbreak, pain and sorrow. Frustration and regret can trap us in a corner, while worry and fear taunt us day in and day out. At times we may feel small and meaningless and to make it even worse, we may feel completely alone. When it gets really bad, sometimes, we can't see a way out of our suffering. We fall in and out of anxiety and depression. We get stuck in our misery and darkness completely paralyzed. Our lives become something we absolutely hate and wish we never had. We compare and become jealous of what others have. Our hearts harden and we become numb to ultimately feeling dead. However, no matter where you are at in your life right now or what you are going through, light can be found in the darkest of times. We all believe something about ourselves. All of us have some kind of faith, even if it's not felt, seen or heard.

It is important to look for and challenge ourselves to find the bigger picture of what life has in store for us. Once it is discovered, a person feels a type of peace they have never felt before. Little things don't seem like huge things anymore and life is given a different meaning. My life is no more important than yours. I am no better than you and you are no better than me. We are all one. We all share the same ability to feel, think and do. We all have feelings and we all have thoughts. More importantly, we all come into this world and leave this world the same way. We are born and then we die. We were all put on this earth for a reason.

When we experience any type of loss, we must learn to reconstruct ourselves from the inside out. We have to be brave and find understanding we will never be the same we once were. One loss actually leads to several other losses. Even though you may be struggling, you must be strong and remember this is your only life. Fight through the pain. We don't get a trial run at life. This is the final game, so raise your attention and strengthen your focus. Don't waste your life away in self-pity and selfishness. Life is a gift, it was given to you. We didn't do anything to earn it. More importantly, you have to ask yourself, "Would my love one want me to live like this?" They would want you to continue living and living your life to the fullest!

I spent over three years of my life consumed in selfishness. My healing began when I finally chose to rise above and face my hardships. I made a choice to figure out a way to get out of my suffering. Every minute counts, please don't do what I did. Use every moment you are given to the best of its abilities. You can do it, I have faith in you.

Break Your Patterns

Your Strength Is Found In Your Weakness

As the days go by, life can become overly habitual. For instance, we take the same roads to work, drink our same coffee every morning, tie our shoes the same way, eat the same things for lunch, brush our teeth the same way, talk to strangers in the same way, order the same things at restaurants and watch the same T.V. shows each night. I bet even some of you have specific sleeping routines you do each night to fall asleep. It is no joke, everyday so many of us run on auto drive and we aren't even conscious of it! Even if we hate admitting it, we are all guilty of it. Unconsciously, patterns rule, run, and steal our lives and people wonder why their lives aren't getting any better.

For grieving people especially, many seem to get stuck in their depressed state and negative routine. It's almost like horse blinders get applied to each side of our eyes and our sight becomes limited. We then have a hard time seeing what's truly out there and our patterns take control.

When hard times come and our focus becomes limited like this, it can be very hard to change. Unless, we know what is going on and what to do to help ourselves. In these times we can get scared, doubtful and anxious and stand there surrounded by life helpless in our tracks. Every day can turn into a day of survival and every night a night of fear and dread for the next day to come. No one deserves to live a life like this. Luckily for us, there is a way out of this suffering.

For life to improve, one must walk by faith and not by sight. One must take steps to break the limiting patterns in their life and replace them with healthy ones. A shield of courage and a sword of honesty has to be used to break yourself free. Our life is our responsibility. No one is truly able to help us like we can help ourselves. So stop waiting for something to happen, be that someone who makes something happen! The power of self-belief, hard work, discipline and constant awareness is key. The quality of our patterns is the quality of our life!

Your faith is not intellectual nor is it emotional. It is spiritual in nature and in times of loss it is tested. You may or may not consider yourself a spiritual person, but call this whatever you want. I truly believe there are forces out there we are incapable of understanding or seeing that hold our universe together, things we can and cannot control and purpose for everything. When we are challenged with hardships in life, faith in ourselves, others and in life is what gets us to the other side. Our faith can be the force used to help us heal.

Loss is a time where an individual can choose to gain

strength in their life. They can take the event that has happened and give it a meaning that will bring massive growth into their life. In order to recover, it's about jumping into the unknown. We have to stop saying, "I'm fine," when we're really not. We need to leave judgement and criticism out of our lives and fill our hearts with compassion and love. Rather than living in a suffering state and seeing only the bad, we must choose to live each day in a beautiful state and see the good in life. Moving beyond loss is about discovering and working towards finishing what life had and has in store for you. The learning and growth never quits! Faith in life and in ourselves is what gets us to where we want to go and is what makes the impossible events in our lives become possible. Your wellbeing and abundance of happiness during life is found from within in this moment right now.

It is time to have a say in what happens and doesn't happen in your life. Don't let your problems rule what you do. When you find yourself running or hiding from them, that is when you must face them! Break the patterns that are stealing your life away. It is time to say, "Enough is enough!" Who knows, you might realize the problems in your life happened for you to make you a stronger and better person. Maybe you will realize they happened in order for you to become who you needed to be or maybe they had nothing to do with you and where out of your control. The meaning you give circumstances in your life and the quality of state you live in are directly related to the quality of your life. What if problems were actually learning experiences for you so you could become who you were meant to be? What if God knew you could handle them so He gave them to you so you could learn how to help others through their pain? What if they were actually gifts? What if there was more to our suffering? When we change our mindset to believing life is for us rather than against us, that is when breakthroughs happen and vibrancy is brought back into our lives.

In times of loss, we all turn to our patterns to help us keep going. If you take some time to pay attention to your heart and mind, you will notice we have patterns of emotions we feel and patterns of thoughts we think. Then going one step further, we have habitual actions we do. We do them over and over because that is what has kept us alive thus far. What if I told you, there was a better way to live life? If you are going through a loss of a loved one, please know I am deeply sorry. Whoever they may have been, I know in my heart they impacted you greatly. All people are truly wonderful. Be grateful for the time you shared with them and all they did for you. Your grief that you are experiencing right now came from a place of love and connection. Each time we choose love we put our hearts on the line for heartbreak. You are brave and you are beautiful. If you are going through a divorce or a job loss, please know I am also deeply sorry. No matter how much they meant or didn't mean to you, remember they happened for a reason. More importantly, just like everything else under the sun, there is a time for joy and a time for pain. This too shall pass.

One of the most efficient techniques to break disempowering habits is to simply stop doing them! It really is that simple, just stop, that's it, but easier said than done right? When you find yourself wanting to do a disempowering action or focusing on an unhelpful emotional or thought pattern, try this four step exercise out;

- First, observe your body language. What are you doing with your body? Are you slouching or is your chest up? Are you stiff and tense or relaxed? Are you breathing deep or shallow? Are you breathing with your stomach or chest? Are you hungry or thirsty? Are you tired or energized?

- Second, observe where all your attention is going. What are you focusing on? Is it positive or negative? Empowering or disempowering? Identify where it is coming from and why are you focusing on that?

- Third, observe the thoughts going on inside your mind. What are you thinking? Are your thoughts positive or negative? Are they helping you and others or hurting you and others? Are they really true? Do you really believe that? Is that really you? Is it coming from a place of love or suffering and stress?

- Fourth, observe your environment. Is your environment giving you pleasure or pain? Is it disempowering or empowering you? Are the people you surround yourself adding value to your life or causing you to suffer? Is the people and place that surround for you or against you? Supportive or unsupportive?

After looking closer from within using these four steps, you will be able to take effective steps that can serve you and life. You will be able to see what needs to be changed, what is hurting and limiting you and what can help and support you. The hurting and stress can all go away. Admitting to yourself the emotions you are feeling and the thoughts going on inside your head are some of the best things you can do for yourself. You will be able to see the moment for what it truly is. You will have the chance to stop doing what you are doing and do something that empowers you. Being honest with yourself about your environment and who you surround yourself with, gives you the advantage to take the steps to clean it up. You will be able to determine if the location you are in or the people you are with are either pushing you farther from where you want to be or pulling you closer to the life you desire. Sunny skies are in the forecast and lasting change is inevitable. It is sometimes in our greatest sorrows that we find the light.

Sticking your finger in your nose, looking into a mirror and smiling at yourself, splashing cold water into your face, doing twenty jumping jacks or laughing hysterically for no reason are all easy ways to interrupt your patterns both physically, emotionally and mentally. I wouldn't be telling you this if I didn't learn from experience how to break my own negative, limiting patterns.

Awareness and willpower is absolutely needed to interrupt and change these types of patterns. When negative emotions and thoughts arise, because they will, let them come up. Feel them and think them as they surface, but learn to not hold onto them or push them away. Let them go when they are done. Allow room so more positive and inspiring ones can come in and impact your soul. Trade a negative emotion and thought for a positive one. When has holding onto or avoiding a negative emotion or thought ever helped someone?

To accomplish this, you need to make a deal with yourself and when I say deal, I mean a real, genuine kind of deal. The deal is so important, it almost means do or die. It requires soldier like honesty and dedication. You have to hold a promise in your heart you will do whatever it takes. Just say yes, get leverage on yourself today and alienate your limiting habits.

So when you start thinking things like, "My life is never going to get better," or "This pain will never go away," ask yourself two questions; Is this thought serving or hurting me? And is it necessarily true? When you realize they aren't serving you, you can take direct action to handle them appropriately. You can then consciously change the thoughts right then and there to, "My life will get better," and "This pain will go away." Once you become aware of things like this, you realize you can no longer take the pain you hold inside. You see how much these types of thoughts have been limiting you and how these types of emotions have been causing you so much pain. That is when you put your foot down and say, "No more!" After you have experienced this a couple of times, you begin to link so much pain to doing the old negative pattern you'd do anything to avoid it. That is what I call leverage! Once you are to that point, you then need to find something to think, feel or do in its place. It is vital to find a new empowering pattern to put in its place so you don't revert to your old ways. And believe me, under extreme stress, that is easy to do.

Trust me, if you dedicate yourself to this and do this daily, it will work! The possibilities are limitless. When my dad died, I struggled with life for years. I lost my purpose, became numb and honestly didn't care if I lived or not. It wasn't until I finally said, "I can't live like this anymore, I must change," that I began to take the steps that I am sharing with you now to heal. I dove deep into my suffering and discovered who I really was.

I may not understand what you are going through, but I am human. I can feel the kinds of emotions you feel and I have the ability to think just like you. We are so different yet so alike. We may have different vehicles and reasons to our emotions, thoughts and beliefs, but we all share one thing in common. We each are given the ability to experience life. We are in this together. We are here for a reason. Know I am here for you. If I can do this, so can you! Choose to rise above your circumstances, you deserve a wonderful life without suffering! If you are at the lowest you have ever been in your entire life, I have good news for you. There is nowhere, but up from here!

Love Is The Greatest Of Them All...

Awaken Your Soul

Loving and accepting one's self is one of the most valuable actions any person can take. This is the foundation of all creation. Love is the basis for success in all areas of life. The kind of relationship we hold with ourselves ultimately determines and expresses the type of person we are. If we don't show and feel love for ourselves, how do we then give love and receive love from others?

If you have ever been on an airplane, you will notice each time before liftoff, the flight attendant gives a speech. And if you have flown multiple times, you probably have recognized the speech is very similar each time. In this speech, flight safety and precautions are addressed. One of the most important topics they talk about is what to do with the oxygen masks in case of an emergency. They give a demonstration on how to correctly release the mask from the overhead and how to put it on. Then while quickly racing through the rest of the script they say, "When placing on the oxygen mask, always remember to apply the mask first to yourself before beginning to help other passengers." Why do you think they say to do that?

In an emergency where danger is imminent, you are useless if you don't help yourself first. By not putting your mask on first, you put yourself at an even greater risk for fainting, injury or even death. What good are you to other passengers if you don't help yourself first?

Living life is actually the same kind of situation. If we don't help and take care of ourselves first, how then can we be of service? Before you can truly love or help someone else, you must first learn to love and help yourself. You must learn to love yourself during the good times and more importantly, the bad ones. No matter what life throws at you, be there for yourself. In the book of Proverbs, King Solomon writes, "To acquire wisdom is to love yourself; people who cherish understanding will prosper." He also writes, "Keep your heart with all vigilance, for from it flow the springs of life." The love you give to yourself will help heal and nurture you. Love mends, love conquers, love strengthens and love lives on forever. It is unconditional, it is sacred and it is eternal. It is what binds everything together in perfect harmony and it is the force that overcomes evil.

You may struggle with low self-esteem, extreme guilt, anger or lack of purpose. Please, don't fear. You are not alone in your vulnerability. Many people, including me, struggle. In times of grief, feelings become more sensitive and intensified. Things are brought to the surface that you never knew existed. Instead of feeling ashamed of who you are and comparing yourself to others, consider taking the time to love yourself. You're you, the only you, so just be you!

Place your hands over your heart, close your eyes and take a deep breath in. Feel the air and your chest rise as you focus on your heart. Be grateful for your mind, body and life. Thank your mind and body for getting you where you are today. Forgive them for all the times they messed up, hurt you, or let you or others down. Say sorry to them for all the times you hurt or were mean to them. Remember, what you are going through isn't you. It is just life. What happened to you is an experience. Life will continue to go on with or without you. The only person you can blame for the way you feel is you. We can't blame others or the experience. You are the one who creates the emotions and thoughts inside not life. You are the only one that can feel or think them and you are the only one who can heal them.

If you are thinking, "This girl doesn't know what she is talking about, she doesn't know what I have been through nor does she understand". I am here to tell you I was just like you. I believed no one could ever understand what I was going through or help me. I felt alone. No one's advice was good enough for me and no one was going to tell me what to do, but can I give you some advice?

If I could go back in time and say something to the

old me, it would go something like this. Stop putting that wall up and trying to protect yourself from life. The only thing you should really be protecting yourself from is yourself. Everybody should work towards being the same person in public that they are alone. There is no one else like you. Realize people are kind creatures and are just trying to help you. They are talking to you with reason. They are trying to help make your life better. If the purpose of life was to be alone and figure it all out on our own, God would have put us in bubbles. He would have separated us, but he didn't. Our sins and being selfish is what separate us. In 1 Corinthians it reads, "Love is patient and kind; love does not envy or boast; it is not arrogant or rude. It does not insist on its own way; it is not irritable or resentful; it does not rejoice at wrongdoing, but rejoices with the truth. Love bears all things, believes all things, hopes all things, and endures all things. Love never ends. As for prophecies, they will pass away; as for tongues, they will cease; as for knowledge, it will pass away." Love is all powerful and all healing.

I can promise you, if you are fully present and take in what others say, not only will it make the grieving process faster, but you will gain the love and happiness you desire. You will become confident in that with whatever you lost, you will be alright without. You will realize you are not alone and you can make it. Pride is the one of the biggest destructors of them all. Learn to control it and say yes to love. Begin to live with openness and an open heart. Put your wall down and begin to find the answers to healing. Love has the power to heal all wounds.

If you lost someone, let that person hold a special place in your heart. Don't let what happened to you make you think you need to change who you are to be happy again. Inside your body, you were the same soul before the loss, during it and now after. You have always been there, through it all. The happiness you desire is found within. You just have to choose to find it, see it and feel it. Dig deep and use the path of love to find it. Love feeds the soul and conquers all!

I have come to realize the heart doesn't necessarily give us life. It is the soul that gives you and I life! Without your soul, there is no heart, no mind or no body. The heart is an instrument that keeps the physical body alive and functioning. For instance, think about heart transplants. A heart transplant is a surgical procedure when a nonfunctional or diseased heart is removed and then a new heart is transplanted into its place. Thousands of people's lives are improved on a daily basis because of this amazing procedure. However, I have one question for you. Do you think the person who got the new heart is the same person after the procedure or do you think they gained a new personality because someone else's heart is now inside of them? The answer is clear, they are the same person they were before and now after the procedure. They have the same personality, likes and dislikes, the same name and the same memories. They are the same soul. Anything is possible when we use our souls. You are the soul that gives life to your world. We are spiritual beings with souls who are having a physical experience.

Just for fun, everyday, look in the mirror at yourself and say 50 times with a smile on your face, "I love you." I promise, it will change your life! You are an amazing human being! I am so thankful for your soul! You are truly incredible!

The Present Moment
Where Do You Live Life From?

In order to gain happiness, people must learn to live in the present moment. So many of us today are either worrying about the future or reliving the past over and over. We let the past and future distort our present. No one seems to schedule time in their day to just focus on the present moment. As a society we are constantly on the go. Why do you think most of us live like this? Is it because the present is not good enough or are we actually afraid of it? Can we not just handle being in the present with ourselves? Is life being too hard on us?

I believe we do this as a survival mechanism to meet our needs. What's heartbreaking, is people don't even realize they are doing it! So many of us are missing out on all the beautiful experiences life is giving us. We choose to see the present with false eyes and not see it for what it really is.

However, we are all innocent. Each day, we all live our lives trying to do the best that we know how. Everyday, people are innocently letting the past overwhelm their attention and the future cause extreme fear, stress and turmoil. The past becomes their identity. I have to admit, I was one of those. It all began to change when I started facing and letting go of the past and learning how to focus on the right now.

When experiencing loss, we must not let our past define our present. If we do, we are fooling ourselves. The past was a part of your life, not a part of you. We must see the moment for what it truly is. We can't use the present to live in our past. Loss is a world of suffering. I have been there and can remember thinking, "This is who I am, the girl whose parents got divorced and the orphan girl who lost her dad when she was twenty one years old." It was my identity and I carried it around with me for years. What happened to the girl in between those two events? Who was she and where did she go? She was a girl who loved to laugh, play sports, sing, hang out with friends, visit the ocean, go to the movies, go shopping and explore the world. What happened to that Shelby?

Being caught in the storm of those two events, I lost sight of my identity along the way. The past became my present and the future became my worst fear. I began to identify with those events and do everything I could to prevent more suffering to occur. I made up an untrue story and caused myself to believe I was a girl with a terrible and sad life. Slowly, I began to shut down. I was in so much pain, I became numb. I began to relive the past over and over and only obsess about the future. I scowled at the idea of the present moment being a "present". I was a hurt little girl who needed to heal. I was a girl playing the victim card instead of the hero in my circumstances. I was afraid and I felt like I was alone. I didn't know who I was or what I would do in the present moment. I felt completely empty. So what did I do? I gave up and almost killed myself. Thankfully, something amazing happened during those dark moments and I chose to fight and live. (If you think hearing that part of my story would help you, message Balance Awakened and I will get in contact with you.)

Do you know what fear stands for? False evidence appearing real. That can't get any truer. Fear is the number one thing that holds people back or causes them to do what they do. We live in a world trying to do everything that gives us pleasure while at the same time, doing anything to avoid things that cause us pain. People are afraid of what will happen or what will not happen.

As people we need to take the necessary steps to face our fears. We have to stop running from them and start dancing with them until they are so tired, they can't dance anymore. Remember, the past experiences you went through are now gone. They are dead. Stop letting the dead control the alive. True reality is found in the present moment. If you change your story and stop letting the past and future dictate your present, you will experience life for what it really is.

Forgive The Person Who Left You

And Find Freedom

Forgiving was one of the hardest things I have ever had to do, but one of the best things I ever did for myself. I spent years caught up in missing my dad. I couldn't let go of him. I longed for his connection, but also had anger stored in my heart. I was mad at him for leaving me. I thought and asked daily, "Why couldn't you have been smarter and not gotten electrocuted? You left us here to suffer and die. My life is ruined." I was absorbed in my suffering and blamed my dad and everyone else for my pain. Years went by and the anger stayed. Over time, my memory of him began to slowly become more imaginative than real. His presence here on earth became harder and harder to feel. My heart was cold and I felt far from comfortable. An emptiness consumed me. It wasn't until one day, I decided to pick up and read my bible.

The bible verse read, "Make allowance for each other's faults, and forgive anyone who offends you. Remember, the Lord forgave you, so you must forgive others. Above all, clothe yourselves with love, which binds us all together in perfect harmony. And let the peace that comes from Christ rule in your hearts. For as members of one body you are called to live in peace. And always be thankful."

That day I realized I needed to forgive my dad, I had

to let go of the blame and anger and I had to free him from my unconscious grudge. I realized forgiving him was not just for him, but it was for me. The power of forgiveness saved my life that day. I tell you this because forgiveness can heal in more ways than you can imagine.

Right now, I am asking you to forgive the person who left you. Life is not meant to be about what it gives to you, but what you give to it and how you respond to it. Reality is reality. It can be mean, unfair, traumatizing and ugly. Sometimes it feels like we're trying to find the eye in the storm, but I am here to tell you, the storms aren't there to kill you. They're there to make you a better swimmer.

You have to find it in your heart to accept it is going to be hard, it might hurt and you'll want to quit at times. You may not fully understand why it had to happen to you or why you lost that special person or pet, but understand God placed it in your path for a reason. You must ask yourself, "Would they want me to be sad or live like this?" Once you see they wouldn't want you to be sad or live the way you are living, make it one of your life missions to live your life in honor of who you lost. Be a better person for the world because of what they did for you.

When the time comes and you think you can't handle anymore, handle just a little more because that is when breakthroughs happen! Don't give up! Remember, the hard times too will pass. Life is what you make it. It can be heaven or hell. The focus and the meaning you give it is key. The quality of your focus is the quality of your life. To find your destiny sometimes you have to jump into your fear and forgive who and what needs forgiven. Sometimes that even means forgiving yourself.

Society Who?

May Your Suffering Bring Redemption

When you type "definition of society" in Google, the first definition that pops up reads, "the aggregate of people living together in a more or less ordered community."

When I read this, the word "ordered" stood out like a sore thumb. How many people do you think live their lives based on the 'orders' and 'expectations' society gives them? How many people do you think are influenced by what others say? In the world today, so much of what we do is influenced by the opinion of others. Me, being one of the guiltiest, fell into this trap. It was a trap that stole my happiness.

I lived my life to please others. I did things to make others happy and seek their approval. I allowed the outside world to control my actions and decisions. I lived so many years of my life trying to meet everyone's expectations and I was far from finding fulfillment in my life. I felt completely empty.

It wasn't until I finally admitted to myself, my identity was based off of society's expectations that I started to find myself again. I allowed society to define my reality. When I put my foot down and became vulnerable to the outside world, that was when things began to change. That was when the real Shelby Doner appeared.

The only thing worse than telling a lie is living a lie.

Like I said, we all should strive to be the same in public that we are alone. Society can be a big bully. It can be hateful, mean and downright dirty, but don't let it take your hope away. Don't let it steal your life or tell you how you should be. Take a step back for a moment and ask yourself, "Is this really who I am? Is this really who I want to be or is this society telling me who I should be?" The questions what, how, why, where and who can begin to reveal who we really are and what we really want out of life.

Don't let the outside world and people's actions or words offend you. When they come, refuse to let them hurt you. Just let them go. When they are held inside, that is when things start to get blurry. We start to get off track and lose our real sense of self. When looking for answers, we should look inside rather than outside. I'll be the first to tell you, "Don't fake it, til you make it!" If you do this you are just hurting yourself and life around you.

For example, don't just work to work. Work for a reason, a reason you are passionate about. They don't say, "Do what makes you happy" for no reason. I talk to and see so many people who live most of their lives stuck in a job they hate. It's not just the poor people who aren't happy. I've met and observed many rich people who are just as unhappy. Robin Williams is a prime example. He took his own life because of it. He seemed to be so focused on making others happy, he forgot to take care of his own happiness along the way and got lost. Like I said, life is short so please make the best of it. If you're doing something that doesn't make you happy, stop doing it! The world we live in is full of abundance and opportunity. Don't take it for granted while you have it. Find a job, a spouse, a home, and a hobby you love. Don't let your doubt or fear get in your way. More importantly, don't let the excuses you tell yourself and others stop you. You deserve happiness, peace, bliss and joy. Sometimes using our hearts rather our minds, can be the best thing we ever do for ourselves. You will be amazed at what you can do when you put your heart into it. You must choose to find and be the happiness you desire. You must be the change you want to see in the world.

Now that we know the acronym for fear, do you know what real stands for? Real evidence appearing lively! The time is now to change the story you have been identifying with for so long. You are not the story you tell yourself over and over. I promise you, there is always going to be a new and better story! You are something far greater than that! You are a being of light, love and joy. You are a part of the force that keeps this world alive. How special you are. You my friend, are an amazing and unique being!

Jesus said, "Treat others how you would want to be treated." Do we do that as a society or do we treat others so we get what we want? What we give in life is what we get. For example, if you don't help others heal, people won't help you heal. You reap what you sow. If we chose to stop feeling sorry for ourselves and instead focus on bigger and better things, our lives would be transformed completely. When you find yourself stuck in your struggles, ask a better question or take action. Focusing solely on ourselves does not change the outcome for anyone nor does it bring us closer to happiness. Getting closer to happiness is about ending the separation and suffering. It is about becoming together as one and sharing. It is truly a beautiful experience when you are happy and you help others find happiness.

When someone says to their spouse, "I want a divorce, I have been cheating on you and am in love with someone else," the first question a person normally asks is, "With who?" This question does more harm than good. Why is this question the first one people ask out of all the other questions one could ask? What good does it do for a person to know who the secret lover was? It actually causes more pain and suffering in the long run because we blame the outside world and others for how we feel inside. Most then begin to become jealous, angry and hateful towards that person and they don't even know them. Depression, envy and emptiness can all set in too along the way.

Depending on the situation instead of asking that first, one could possibly ask, "What else could this mean or why did this happen?" Of course what the betrayer did was disrespectful and unfaithful, but you must look out for yourself! Remember, the only person a person can completely control is themselves. One must learn to respond rather react in times of loss.

Demanding for a higher truth in any situation is beneficial. Suffering blinds our sight as easily as a blindfold, but who said we have to suffer for so long? It is our responsibility to get out of our own suffering. We must admit to ourselves what we are holding inside is taking from our quality of life. Stop letting the ego tell you what to do. I know every single being on this earth has some kind of good in them.

Good is in our nature, but why do you think people do what they do? Why is their good and evil? At the center of it all, we all do what we do because we want to feel okay inside, have happiness and live a fulfilling life. People do what they do in search of it and for protection of it.

If being bigger than your problems was easy, everybody would take the steps to overcome them. Most try, but then quit. Others on the flipside, actually like to hold onto their pain and suffering for personal gain. We may lose some, but we can gain so much more. It is called sacrifice. Because you picked up this book and are reading it right now, I know you are one of those people who do not want to be controlled by their problems. You are in search for a more purposeful, meaningful, loving and amazing life! You want to be happy, AWESOME! I can tell you have a winner's heart and I am here to tell you, you will get it!

It's important to always remember to not be so easily influenced. One should always be aware of what he or she is doing and what is going on around them. He or she should always reflect before acting and see if they are coming from a place of love or hate. God gave you a soul and he gave you a mind for a reason. Use your soul to use the mind effectively! It is very easy to become addicted to our emotional patterns. If something is not changing or working, take the time to investigate. Instead of worrying about the how, ask why. The quality of your decisions is the quality of your life. The quality of your emotions is the quality of your life. We can't just sit here and keep waiting for a miracle to happen. If you want more, you must do something about it. You must break your habits and addictions. Life is about experiencing and learning. If you need help, ask for it! If we knew it all and accomplished everything, what would be the point of it?

You are worthy enough, you are good enough and you are not a failure. Please don't let the illusion of rejection and shame ruin your life. Let them go and remember the only true opinion that matters is yours.

Our suffering is not a denial of life, but a confirmation of it. It is in our suffering we find life. Loss and death are at work in us and life is for us. Suffering can actually lead us to a greater life that will not only serve ourselves, but others. Our biggest devastations can become our redemptions. Life is not against us. Loss has the power to enhance our joy, our love and our character. In the bible it reads, "For our light and momentary troubles are achieving for us an eternal glory that far outweighs them all." By reading this, I pray it gives you hope and encouragement.

One Choice

Say Yes

What do you think the difference is between a happy person and a sad person? What has to happen in order for a person to feel and be fulfilled? Why are some people naturally strong and some are weak? Why are we all so different yet so alike? Why is there suffering? Specifically, what has to happen for a person to get through grief?

I want to remind you, we are all fascinating, strong, creative and brilliant beings. What we have and can achieve is amazing. We are incredible, I mean, think about it! We found a way to travel in the air and created a way to fly into outer space! We have created medicine that heals sickness and we are pretty good at making music too. My question is, how and why do you think this was all achieved? It is because human beings believed they could do it.

If you think you can do something, you can, but if you think you can't, you can't and won't. A person who says, "I can," and another who says "I can't do it," are both usually right. What we hold in our mind tends to manifest. And more importantly, sometimes what we hold in our mind, is far from the truth.

Are your thoughts hurting or serving you? Are you thinking more negatively or positively? Is what you are thinking really what happened? Is it true?

The power of belief and mindset is key to our survival. It determines the quality and ultimately the end outcome of our lives. Don't let terrible and uncomfortable experiences ruin the rest of your life. More importantly, don't let external factors control you. You have to make the choice to make a change in your life. You have to choose to give it all a different, empowering meaning. The power lies within your own hands. Be confident and courageous, it is your choice to make. The journey may seem unpredictable and frightening at times, but remember, you don't need to know the entire journey. You just need to know the next best step. When you figure that out, take it! Believe in yourself and walk on water! Make the impossible become possible! You can win this fight! You are just as much of a human being as the ones described above.

While you are on your journey, remember you are never alone. We all have struggles and shortcomings. No one is or has it perfect. Getting support and help from another is one of the best things a person can do for themselves. Stop letting your pride get in your way. Your pain is no different than someone else's. Support groups are magical and self-help books are beautiful. Hearing other people's stories restores hope. Asking for help from another and become a person of service for others. It is one of the strongest cures to all types of grief. Give yourself grace and have faith. You will get through this. I believe in you!

During my grief, I realized I absolutely hated myself and was faking it just to make it. I let the world and the past tell me how my life should be. I was tired of it all and knew my negative patterns were killing me slowly. I mean I was at the brink of killing myself when I decided to stand back up and make a change. I knew I had a choice to make. In that complete darkness, that was when I took my next step. Maybe you too will see the light in your darkness and take that next step.

One of the greatest things I ever did for myself was make myself accountable for my life and actions. I wrote a commitment letter to myself. I made it a priority to do whatever it took to heal. I became more honest with myself than I had ever been before. I chose to face, stop and learn to control my suffering. But most importantly, I chose to find happiness again. I chose to find and become the person I wanted to be. I chose to start being the same person I am in public that I am when I am alone with myself. I decided to be me and give myself the love I needed. I became committed, disciplined, consistent, hopeful and courageous. With genuine action, grace and patience, I began to slowly heal. I wouldn't be writing this today if I hadn't made those choices. They were truly life transforming.

Every moment we get, is a chance to become better. Your honesty and transparency will lead to your healing. They will lead you to your transformation. You will have peace and you will have an overabundance of happiness in your life if you look from within. Choose not just to survive in life, choose to thrive! Save yourself before it's too late! You must be the change you want in your life and the change you want for this world. I promise you, if you do this, life will never be the same. God bless you and I wish you nothing but the best on your journey. Thank you taking the time to read this.

Yours Truly,
Shelby Doner

P. S. If you would like to connect with Shelby Doner, please go to www.balanceawakened.com or contact her at balanceawakened@gmail.com.

Acknowledgements

This book began as a spark of a moment kind of a thing. It actually came to me during an amazing boat ride in the Grand Canyon. It required more than just my brain and fingers to create and type it up.

First, thank you to my sexy, exuberant husband, Drew. You have been by my side through it all. You have stuck by me in my darkest moments. You never hesitate to help me and you continue to love me unconditionally. Your consistent feedback and encouragement is indispensable. I love you. Thank you.

Second, thank you to my brother, Luke, and sisters, Alyssa and Jadyn. It has been a joy to grow up with you all. You too have been by my side through it all. Your guys' bravery, honesty and genuineness is something so special to me. Our phone conversations will never get old. Luke, your drive to serve others, to grow and to help make this world a better place, inspire me to be a better person each day. Alyssa, your soft and loving heart and connection with horses, inspire me to love even more. Jadyn, your strength, care for others and bubbly personality even in what seems like the worst of times, inspire me to give everything I can to life. You all make life so much more fun. I am blessed to experience it with you. Thank you.

Thirdly, to my mom, Kelli. It seems like it has been an uphill battle for so long, but I think we finally made it. You will always be my mom. I am thankful for every event in our lives we have shared. I wouldn't be who I am today without you. Dad actually did something right when he married you. I know it didn't work out, but look how much good came from it. I may have hated you when I was young, but I love you more than ever now. Please, forgive me for all my hatefulness and wrongdoings towards you. I am truly sorry. You are one of the strongest human beings I have ever had the privilege of knowing. I honor you and am blessed to call you mom. Thank you.

Fourthly, to all the wonderful people who decided to read my book, thank you. The emails I've received inspire and humble me. Your honesty, courage, stories, and willingness to open up to me, give me appreciation. I am so grateful to connect with you and share this world with you. You all will hold a special place in my heart. You motivate me to continue to strive to help others through their hard times and serve something higher than myself. Thank you.